VICTORIAN LIFE

VICTORIAN TRANSPORT

KATRINA SILIPRANDI

Wayland

VICTORIAN LIFE

A VICTORIAN CHRISTMAS

A VICTORIAN FACTORY

A VICTORIAN HOLIDAY

A VICTORIAN SCHOOL

A VICTORIAN STREET

A VICTORIAN SUNDAY

VICTORIAN CLOTHES

VICTORIAN TRANSPORT

HOW WE LEARN ABOUT THE VICTORIANS

Queen Victoria reigned from 1837 to 1901, a time when Britain went through enormous social and industrial changes. We can learn about Victorians in various ways. We can still see many of their buildings standing today, we can look at their documents, maps and artefacts – many of which can be found in museums. Photography, invented during Victoria's reign, gives us a good picture of life in Victorian Britain. In this book you will see what Victorian life was like through some of this historical evidence.

Series design: Pardoe Blacker Ltd
Editor: Sarah Doughty
Picture research: Liz Miller

First published in 1993 by Wayland (Publishers) Ltd,
61 Western Road, Hove, East Sussex BN3 1JD, England

© Copyright 1993 Wayland (Publishers) Ltd

British Library Cataloguing in Publication Data
Siliprandi, Katrina
  Victorian Transport. - (Victorian Life Series)
  I. Title II. Series
  388.0941

ISBN 0 7502 0846 5

Printed and bound in Great Britain by B.P.C.C Paulton Books Ltd

Cover picture: Victorian horse and carriage.

Picture acknowledgements:
Aberdeen University Library (George Washington Wilson Collection. Ref A123) 21 (top); Batsford 4; The Boat Museum 6 (top); British Waterways 5 (bottom), 6 (bottom); E.T Archive *cover*; Mary Evans 10 (top), 11, 12, 21 (bottom), 23, 25 bottom (Fawcett Library); Glasgow Museums: Museum of Transport 17 (bottom), 24; Howarth-Loomes Collection 10 (bottom); Image Select (Ann Ronan) 26; Jarrold Publishing 22 (top); London Transport Museum 15, 16, 17 (top), 18, 19 (bottom); Billie Love Historical Collection 13 (bottom); Manchester Ship Canal 5 (top); Mansell Collection 9 (bottom), 13 (top), 20, 27 (bottom); Hugh McKnight Photography 7; National Railway Museum 8, 9 (top); The National Tramway Museum 19 (top); Quadrant Picture Library 27 (top); Royal Institution of Cornwall 22 (bottom); Rural History Centre, University of Reading 14 (bottom); Science Museum Library 25 (top).

CONTENTS

MOVING
PEOPLE AND GOODS

Today many people travel long distances, using different kinds of transport. But at the beginning of Queen Victoria's reign there were few types of transport available. Trains, motor buses and cars had not yet been invented. Most people did not go far from home and used their feet to move from place to place.

TRANSPORTING GOODS

Walking to market.

If you were a farmer with animals to sell, you would have to walk along rough roads to market. If you were a factory owner and needed supplies of coal to power machinery, you would usually have to rely on horses and carts to deliver them. Transporting goods in early Victorian times was difficult, unless you were lucky enough to live near a river or canal where you could use boats or barges.

Many of the canals the Victorians used were built at the end of the eighteenth century before the Victorian period began.

DIGGING CANALS

New canals were also built during Victorian times. The men shown in this picture are called navvies or cutters. They are using spades to cut out a new canal.

Canals like these were used to carry goods to mills and factories. Coal, wool, grain, wood and iron were all moved on canal boats. By the 1850s, more than 3,000 km of canals had been built in Britain. It was possible to travel across Scotland by canal. In England, canal boats could travel from Sussex in the south to Yorkshire in the north.

Navvies in the nineteenth century.

CANAL LOCKS

Sometimes locks needed to be built if a canal was to run across hilly areas of land. They were used to raise or lower boats from one level to another. Most locks were 22 m long and just over 2 m wide. Many boats were specially built to fit into the locks. They were called narrow boats. If the canal went upwards very steeply several locks had to be built. This was called a flight of locks.

A lock.

CANAL BOAT

In the first half of Queen Victoria's reign, most canal boats were pulled by horses. The horse walked on a path beside the canal in front of the boat. The path was called a towpath. The horse towed the boat along at the end of a rope. The boat in the picture, *Tiger*, is a barge on the Leeds and Liverpool canal. It is wider than a narrow boat.

Some boats went through canal tunnels. Most canal tunnels did not have a towpath. People called leggers lay on their backs on planks of wood which stuck out from the sides of the boat. They put their feet against the tunnel walls and 'walked' along them, pushing the boat forward.

The Leeds and Liverpool canal boat *Tiger*.

LIFE ON A NARROW BOAT

Two restored and decorated narrow boats.

Most narrow boat families had to live on board their boats. They lived in a tiny cabin that was about 2 m wide and less than 3 m long. The children helped with the horses. Not many of them went to school. From about 1870 many narrow boats were brightly painted like the ones at the bottom of page 6.

STEAM CANAL BOAT

A steam canal cruiser.

From the 1880s, some canal boats used steam engines instead of horses to power them. Canals became less important for carrying goods because railways were cheaper and quicker. Canals were built by different companies. They put up iron name-plates along the towpath. Bridges over the canals also had iron or stone signs. Near the canals there were signposts and markers showing how far it was to the town. Look out for these signs if you are near a canal.

RAILWAY TRAVEL

During the eighteenth century, steam became more important as a source of power. In 1804 a steam railway engine was tested successfully. In 1825 the first proper railway opened. A huge number of railways were built in Victorian Britain. It meant that people and goods could travel much faster, more cheaply and in all weather conditions.

The railway carriage used by Queen Victoria.

QUEEN VICTORIA'S CARRIAGE

Queen Victoria first travelled on a train in 1842. At that time there were 2,988 km of railway track in Britain. By the end of the Victorian era, this had been extended to about 35,000 km. Queen Victoria enjoyed travelling by train and often used it to go to her home at Balmoral Castle in Scotland. She spent many holidays there. You can see from this picture of Queen Victoria's railway carriage that it has been furnished to make it especially comfortable.

THE COST OF RAILWAYS

Building a railway was expensive. To raise the money, a company was formed. The company sold shares to anyone who wished to buy them. In return each person who owned shares was given part of the profit that the railway made. At first people made a lot of money from railway shares. Later, some of the companies went broke and people no longer wanted to buy the shares.

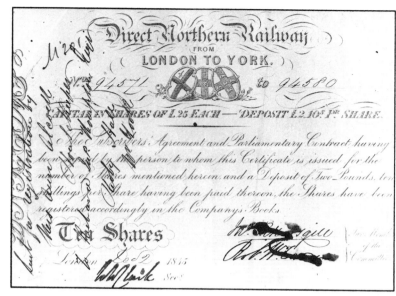

Railway shares, 1845.

RAILWAY ACCIDENTS

Building a railway was very dangerous work. Over a hundred men, or navvies, were killed building the railway between London and Bristol which stretched for about 160 km. In Victorian times, there were many railway accidents.

In this picture from 1866, a collapsed bridge has caused a goods train to derail. In 1879, the Tay bridge in Scotland blew down, six months after Queen Victoria travelled across it. All the eighty passengers were killed.

A railway accident near Beckenham.

RAILWAYS

This is Victoria station in London. Stations in cities were often built with high glass roofs. At busy times the stations became very dirty and smoky.

The railways encouraged more people to live in towns. Food for people and materials for industries were brought to towns by railways. Rich people used railways to travel to work and to go on holiday. Poor people could not afford to go on holiday, but they used the railways for a day out. They might go for a trip to the seaside or into the countryside.

Victoria station, about 1894.

RAILWAY CARRIAGES

Third-class carriage.

Victorian trains had first, second and third-class carriages. This picture shows a third-class carriage, which was the cheapest way to travel. In early Victorian times, many third-class carriages did not even have a roof. Before the 1880s, there was no heating on trains. Porters provided footwarmers for passengers at every station. Trains were lit by oil or paraffin lamps. In the 1880s, gas lights were introduced.

RAILWAY SERVANTS

Can you see some of the people who worked for the railway in this picture? They were called railway servants. Their different uniforms give you clues about their jobs. Railway companies sometimes provided homes for their workers. These railway buildings are often still used for housing even if the railway has since closed.

Holiday-makers returning to Waterloo station.

HORSES AND TRACTION ENGINES

In Victorian times, horses were used for pulling goods and passengers. People also rode horses to get from one place to another. Today, there are as many horses in Britain as there were in the nineteenth century but we use them for leisure rather than transport. The development of steam power meant that some of the heavy jobs done by horses could now be done by machines.

STAGE COACH

In 1837, there were stage coaches like these on the roads. They travelled long distances and carried passengers, parcels and the post. Only rich people could afford to ride on stage coaches. These coaches are in the courtyard of an inn.

A Victorian stage coach.

Passengers booked their seats at the inn. They could have food and drink while they waited for the coach to begin their journey. Coaches could change horses at the inn. Railways put an end to long-distance stage coaches. Travel by train was faster, cheaper and more comfortable.

CARRIER'S WAGON

Before railways were built, the cheapest way to travel was by carrier's wagon. These wagons carried mainly goods and parcels. They were much slower than stage coaches. They were usually drawn by teams of eight horses, sometimes more. The carrier walked or rode alongside, carrying a long carrier's whip. The wagons had very wide wheels so that they did not damage the road with their heavy loads.

Carrier's wagon and horses.

HORSE AND CARRIAGE

A family on their way to a funeral.

In the countryside, people often travelled on horseback. Horses could be changed at inns. This meant a long distance could be travelled quite quickly. Rich people owned their own carriages and horses. For special events, like weddings and funerals, poorer people hired a horse and carriage. Sometimes a horse and carriage was hired by people to collect someone from the railway station. Glasgow, in Scotland had a station bus which took visitors from the station to their hotel.

HORSE AND CART

Horses were used for transporting crops on farms. They did lots of other work on the farm too. This horse is pulling a wagon that is being loaded with hay.

Horses were also used to pull wagons and carts delivering goods to people. Coal, milk, ice, bread and meat were all delivered by horse and cart.

Harvesting, about 1900.

Traction engine at work.

TRACTION ENGINE

After 1860, traction engines were often used to move heavy loads, such as this enormous log. Traction engines worked by steam and, for a few tasks, they replaced the work of horses. The steam traction engines were only allowed to travel at 6 kph in the countryside and 3 kph through villages and towns.

HORSE-DRAWN BUS

In Victorian times, people in towns could travel on buses pulled by horses. Horse-drawn buses were first used in London in 1829. They were expensive, so only richer people could use them. It cost 5p to travel about 5 km. A conductor collected the fares. He was paid 20p a day. By the late 1840s buses had bench seats along the roof. Bus drivers were paid about 30p a day. They worked from 7.45 am until about midnight. Here are some of a driver's duties:

...not to gallop the horses
...to drive slowly, or at a walk in the markets and in the narrow streets
...to drive at least three feet from the houses, where there is no footpath.

The conductor on a horse-drawn bus in London.

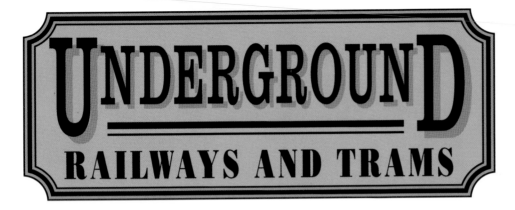

UNDERGROUND
RAILWAYS AND TRAMS

As more goods and passengers came into towns, road traffic became a big problem. By the 1850s it often took longer to cross central London than to travel up to the city by train from Brighton, 80 km away. One answer was to build underground railways. These linked mainline stations with the city centre.

Building an underground railway by 'cut and cover' construction.

BUILDING AN UNDERGROUND RAILWAY

The first underground railway in the world opened in London in 1863. The trains were pulled by steam engines. In the picture you can see an underground railway being built. A wide trench was dug and the track was laid. Then the trench was roofed over. This was called 'cut and cover' construction. Any houses in the path of the railway had to be pulled down. Roads had to be dug up and then rebuilt.

COACH CARS

An underground railway coach.

Later, people found ways to tunnel underground through soft earth. Underground railways built like this were called tube railways. They meant that workers did not have to dig a trench. The first one opened in London in 1890. It worked by electricity instead of by steam engine. The coaches of an underground railway were called cars. This car was nicknamed the 'padded cell'. Can you see why?

HOW THE TRAINS MOVED

This is a poster advertising the first underground cable railway, which opened in Glasgow, Scotland in 1896. A tunnel was built under the city. Thick steel ropes, called cables, were laid through the tunnel. The cables were joined to an engine. This made them move at about 24 kph. Trains gripped on to the cables to move. To stop, they let go of the cable.

A Glasgow subway poster.

The underground cable railway was successful in Glasgow, but apart from some in Europe, few other cable railways were developed.

TRAMS

Trams were introduced in the early 1860s as another new kind of transport in Victorian Britain. A tramway is like a railway, but runs along the road. The tramcar runs on wheels along rails. A tramcar running on smooth iron rails could be pulled much more easily than a horse bus. This is because the wheels of a bus would be moving on a rough, uneven road. Two horses could pull a tramcar with 50 passengers. But two horses could only pull a bus with 25 passengers. At first the rails stuck up above the road. This was dangerous for other road users. After 1869, all the rails were built level with the road.

CONDUCTOR

A conductor sold tickets on the tramcar. He wore a smart uniform. The usual fare was less than 1p for about 3 km. Tramway companies had to sell cheap tickets for working people in the early morning and after 6 pm. Most people could afford to ride on trams. If you wanted to ride on a tramcar you could stop it anywhere in the street.

STEAM TRAMS

In later Victorian times, steam was used instead of horses to move the trams. It was cheaper than using horses and the trams could go faster. Steam trams could not stop as easily as horse trams, so tram stops were introduced. In 1885, an electric tramway started in Blackpool. London's first electric tramway opened in the year Queen Victoria died, 1901.

Advertisement for the Bell Punch ticket machine.

A model steam tram.

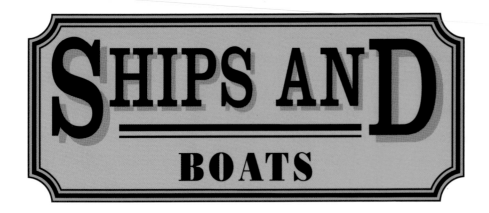

SHIPS AND BOATS

Canals are waterways that have been specially made. But natural waterways were also important for transport. In Victorian Britain, people and goods travelled on rivers and across seas. Sailing ships remained important for trade during Victorian times.

SAILING SHIPS

The biggest and fastest sailing ships were built in Victorian times. They were called clippers. The first clippers were made in the USA. British shipbuilders improved them by making the hulls out of iron instead of wood. This meant they cost less and could carry more cargo. Clippers were mostly used to carry tea from China and wool from Australia.

A clipper called the *Cutty Sark.*

CARGO CARRIERS

At the beginning of Queen Victoria's reign some cargo was carried by steamships. They had paddle wheels turned by a steam engine. Steamships did not need the wind to travel. But they could not carry as much cargo as clippers. In 1838, the first successful steamship with a propeller was made. This was faster than a paddle steamer and more balanced.

In 1869 the Suez canal was built, but there was not enough wind for clippers to use the canal. After this, more and more cargoes were carried by steamships. But this photograph, taken in 1882, shows that sailing ships remained important during Victorian times.

Aberdeen harbour, 1882.

THE 'GREAT EASTERN'

Until the 1880s, steamships had sails in case the engine broke down or the coal ran out. This ship had a propeller, sails and paddle wheels. It was designed by a famous Victorian engineer called Isambard Kingdom Brunel. It was finally launched in 1858. The boat could travel up to 14 knots (26 kph), and carry 4,000 passengers.

The *Great Eastern* steamship.

WHERRIES

On the right is a picture of a boat called a wherry. In Victorian times, wherries carried goods on the waterways of Norfolk and Suffolk. The mast was further forward than on other boats so it could be lowered easily when the wherry came to a bridge. There was only one sail. It was painted black with a mixture of tar and herring oil.

In other parts of Britain, different types of boats developed. See if you can find out if there were any special boats near your home.

A wherry.

FERRIES

King Harry's ferry, 1880s.

Where roads need to cross rivers, bridges are usually built. But in the Victorian times there was far less traffic on the roads than there is today, so it was not always worth building a bridge. It could also be difficult for boats with masts to pass under bridges. Instead, ferries were used to cross rivers in some places. Some ferries could carry horses and carriages as well as people. The ferry was rowed or poled across the water as in the picture at the bottom of page 22.

Henley Regatta, 1893.

HENLEY REGATTA

These people are having fun on the river. This is a picture of the Henley Royal Regatta in 1893. Henley is on the River Thames. Rich people went to watch boats racing. When the racing was over they had a chance to row and pole. Look at the clothes they are wearing. The straw hats with bands were called boaters. Poor people who lived near the river could sometimes go on a Sunday outing on the water.

BICYCLES

AND CARS

Most transport changes in Victorian Britain affected rich people before poor people. At first, bicycles were too expensive for poor people to buy. Until the 1880s, cycling was a hobby for the rich.

HOBBYHORSE

Before Queen Victoria's reign began, a bicycle called the hobbyhorse was invented. The rider moved it by pushing with his or her feet along the ground. This picture shows a copy of the first bicycle to have pedals. It was built by a Dumfries blacksmith called Kirkpatrick Macmillan in 1839. But the idea did not spread. But in 1868 a bicycle called the velocipede became very popular. It was nicknamed the 'boneshaker'. Do you think it sounds like a comfortable ride?

A replica Macmillan bicycle.

PENNY FARTHING

This bicycle is called an ordinary (sometimes known as the penny farthing). Two hundred thousand of these were made between 1870 and 1885. The ordinary was quicker, lighter and more comfortable than the velocipede. But it was difficult to ride. A writer called Flora Thompson described these new bicycles. She wrote 'How fast those new bicycles travelled and how dangerous they looked! ...it was thrilling to see a man hurtling through space on one high wheel, with another tiny wheel wobbling helplessly behind.'
You had to be very fit to ride an ordinary. It was especially difficult for women because of their long skirts.

The ordinary bicycle, or penny farthing.

ROVER SAFETY BICYCLE

In 1885 the Rover safety bicycle was produced. It had a chain to the back wheel. The wheels were the same size. It was much safer than the ordinary. Victorians could buy one for less than £10. By 1895, 800,000 safety bicycles had been made.

Riding a safety bicycle.

RIDING BICYCLES

Rich people bought new safety bicycles. Poorer people bought them second-hand. Many people could afford this form of transport. Some people went to bicycle lessons. These cost between 12½p and 25p for half an hour. A writer called Rudyard Kipling wrote, 'The spring of '96 saw us in Torquay ... everybody was learning to ride things called bicycles. In Torquay there was a circular cinder-track where, at stated hours, men and women rode solemnly round on them. Tailors supplied special costumes for this sport.'

Lots of new shops opened selling bicycles and spare parts. People used bicycles to get to work. In towns and villages shopkeepers used them to deliver goods to their customers.

Learning to ride.

THE MOTOR CAR

Near the end of Victorian times there was a new type of transport on the road. This was the motor car. The first successful petrol driven car was made in Germany in 1885. Cars were very expensive. One like this would cost about £125. Only rich people could buy them. The first cars looked like carriages. The roads were very dusty, so people wore special clothes for driving. Men wore goggles to keep the dust out of their eyes. Women wore a veil over their faces.

A Benz car, from 1898.

A street scene, making fun of the red flag.

THE RED FLAG

Until 1896, someone had to walk in front of the car with a red flag. The red flag was to warn people that a car was approaching. This picture is making fun of the flag. In Victorian times there were very few cars on the road. But the car was a sign of great changes in transport in the future.

TIME LINE

1830s

1837 Queen Victoria's reign began.

1839 K. Macmillan built the first bicycle with pedals.

1840s

1840 First buffet on a station, at Wolverton.

1841 The Great Western railway opened.

1842 Queen Victoria first travelled on a train.

1844 Act of Parliament forced railway companies to provide at least one train a day for third-class passengers over every line. All carriages had to be roofed.

1846 Parliament passed the Gauge Act, forbidding the construction of railways with non-standard gauges.

1850s

1855 Steam tugs introduced on Regent's canal in London.

1858 Brunel's *Great Eastern* floated.

1859 Brunel's bridge across the River Saltash completed.

1860s

1860 First train guard was employed.

1861 First experimental street tramway service introduced in London.

1863 First underground railway opened in London.

1867 Suez canal completed. It opened in 1869.

1000		1500					2000
1066		1485	1603	1714	1837	1901	

MIDDLE AGES

NORMANS

TUDORS

STUARTS

GEORGIANS

VICTORIANS

20TH CENTURY

1870s

1870 J. Sturley designed a high-wheeled bicycle called the ordinary.

1873 North British Railway introduced sleeping cars on the east coast route from London to the north.

1875 Anderton lift built near Northwich, Cheshire. This lifted boats from the river to the canal.

1879 Dining car service introduced on the Great Northern Railway.

1880s

1884 Rover safety bicycle invented. It became successful a year later.

1885 Karl Benz produced the first successful petrol driven car.

First regular steam tramway service introduced.

1888 J. Dunlop invented the pneumatic cycle tyre which was filled with air.

Gottlieb Daimler built the first successful four-wheeled car.

1890s

1890 Forth rail bridge built.

First electric underground railway opened in London.

1892 The Great Western Railway introduced a carriage with toilets.

1894 Manchester Ship Canal opened.

1896 Speed limit increased to 20 kph on the road

Glasgow District Subway opened.

1900s

1901 First electric tram services in London.

Queen Victoria died.

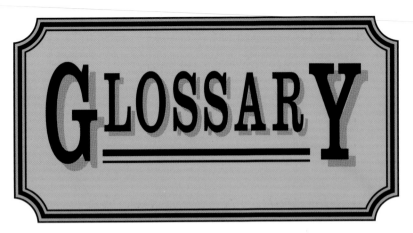

GLOSSARY

Barge A boat used for moving goods.

Canals Waterways that have been built by people.

Cargo The goods carried by a ship or boat.

Company A group of people who join together for business.

Construction The act of building. The word can also mean a building.

Engineers People who can design, construct or maintain anything mechanical.

Footwarmer A metal can that held a chemical called 'hypo' which slowly gave off heat.

Hull The main body of a ship.

Lock Part of a canal closed off by gates. The gates are opened to let the boats pass through.

Navvy A worker who dug canals, and later, railways. The name comes from the word navigator.

Profit When something is sold for more than it cost to buy, the extra money gained is called the profit.

Propeller A shaft with a spiral of blades used to push a boat through the water.

Regatta An event when boats such as yachts or rowing boats take part in races on the water.

Tailor Someone whose job is making clothes.

Tar A thick, sticky mixture, usually used for surfacing roads.

Suez canal A canal that links the Mediterranean Sea with the Red Sea.

Traction engine A steam powered locomotive used for pulling heavy loads along rough roads.

Veil A thin see-through piece of cloth that can be worn over the face.

BOOKS TO READ

Harris, S. *Finding Out About Railways* (Batsford, 1982)

Hudson, K. *Clues to Yesterday's Transport* (The Bodley Head, 1984)

Lines, C. *Exploring Transport* (Wayland, 1988)

Macdonald, F. *A Nineteenth Century Railway Station* (Simon & Schuster Young Books, 1990)

Pace, C. & Birch, J. *Look Around Transport* (Wayland, 1989)

Woodlander, D. *Canals* (A & C Black, 1983)

Young, C. & Miles, J. C. & King, C. *Ships, Sailors and the Sea* (Usborne, 1988)

PLACES TO VISIT

Many museums have transport collections. Here are just a few of them:

ENGLAND

Avon: Bristol Industrial Museum, Prince's Wharf, Prince Street, Bristol, BS1 4RN. Tel: 0272 251470

Birmingham: Birmingham Museum of Science and Industry, Newhall Street, B3 1RZ. Tel: 021 235 1661

Birmingham Railway Museum, 670 Warwick Road, Tyseley, B11 2HL. Tel: 021 707 4696

Cheshire: The Boat Museum, Dockyard Road, Ellesmere Port, South Wirral, L65 4EF. Tel: 051 355 5017

County Durham: The North of England Open Air Museum, Beamish Hall, Beamish, Stanley, DH9 0RG. Tel: 0207 231811

Derbyshire: The National Tramway Museum, Crich, Matlock, DE4 5DP. Tel: 0773 852565

Devon: Exeter Maritime Museum, The Haven, Exeter, EX2 8DT. Tel: 0392 58075

Morwellham Quay Open Air Museum, Morwellham, near Tavistock, PL19 8JL. Tel: 0822 832766

Dorset: Bournemouth Transport and Rural Museum, Transport Depot, Mallard Road, Bournemouth.

Gloucestershire: National Waterways Museum, Llanthony Warehouse, The Docks, Gloucester, GL1 2EH. Tel: 0452 307009

Hampshire: National Motor Museum, John Montagu Building, Beaulieu, Brockenhurst, S04 7ZN.

Lincolnshire: National Cycle Museum, Brayford Wharf, North Lincoln, LN1 1YW. Tel: 0522 545091

London: National Maritime Museum, Romney Road, Greenwich, SE10 9NF. Tel: 081 858 4422

Science Museum, Exhibition Road, South Kensington, SW7 2DD. Tel: 071 938 8000

Transport Museum, 39 Wellington Street, Covent Garden, WC2E 7BB. Tel: 071 379 6344

Merseyside: City of Liverpool Museums, William Brown Street, Liverpool, L3 8EN. Tel: 051 355 5017

The Boat Museum, Dockyard Road, Ellesmere Port, South Wirral, L65 4EF.

Southport Railway Centre, Derby Road, PR9 0TY. Tel: 0704 530693

Norfolk: Bressingham Steam Museum, Bressingham, Diss, IP22 2AB. Tel: 0379 88 382

Maritime Museum for East Anglia, 25 Marine Parade, Great Yarmouth, NR20 2EN. Tel: 0493 842267

The Thursford Collection, Thursford Green, near Fakenham, NR21 OAS. Tel: 0328 878477

North Humberside: Hull Transport and Archaeology Museum, 36 High Street, Hull, HU1 1NQ. Tel: 0482 593902

Hull Maritime Museum, Pickering Park, Hessle Road, Hull, Humberside.

Northamptonshire: The Canal Museum, Stoke Bruerne, near Towcester, NN12 7SE. Tel: 0604 862229

Nottingham: The Canal Museum, Canal Street, Nottingham. Tel: 0602 598835

Shropshire: Ironbridge Gorge Museum, Southside, Church Hill, Ironbridge, Telford.

Suffolk: East Anglian Transport Museum, Chapel Road, Carlton Colville, Lowestoft, NR33 8BL. Tel: 0502 518459

West Midlands: Black Country Museum, Tipton Road, Dudley, DY1 4SQ. Tel: 021 557 9643

North Yorkshire: National Railway Museum, Leeman Road, York, Y02 4XJ. Tel: 0904 621261

West Yorkshire: Bradford Industrial Museum and Horses at Work, Moorside Road, Eccleshill, Bradford, BD2 3HP. Tel: 0274 631756

West Yorkshire Transport Museum, Ludlam Street Depot, Mill Lane, off Manchester Road, Bradford, BD5 0HG. Tel: 0274 736006

SCOTLAND

Lothian: Linlithgow Union Canal Society Museum, Manse Road, EH49 6HQ. Tel: 0506 842289

Strathclyde: Glasgow Museum of Transport, Kelvin Hall, 1 Bunhouse Road, Glasgow G3 8PZ. Tel: 041 357 3929

WALES

South Glamorgan: Welsh Industrial and Maritime Museum, Bute Street, Cardiff, CF1 6AN. Tel: 0222 481919

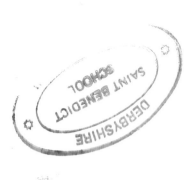